THE VALLEY — BIGGIN HILL

Grandfather's
Biggin Hill

JOHN NELSON

THE LONDON BOROUGH

BROMLEY LIBRARIES 2010

FIRST PUBLISHED IN 1982
by
The author

SECOND EDITION PUBLISHED IN 2010
by
Bromley Libraries
Central Library
High Street
Bromley BR1 1EX
020 8461 7170

ISBN 978 0 901002 22 8

Printed and bound in Great Britain by
CPI Antony Rowe, Chippenham and Eastbourne

CONTENTS

PREFACE TO THE ORIGINAL EDITION

MY GRANDFATHER, William Henry Nelson, was a professional photographer; that was something I knew from an early age. I remember that in the writing desk at our old family home there was once a bundle of the Biggin Hill view postcards which had been left over from his business after his death in 1926, but they were used up well before the end of the Second World War. How I wish I still had them today. Apart from those postcards there was never a suggestion in the family that anything connected with grandfather's work had survived. Not that I ever enquired, since photography held no fascination for me in my younger days.

In the autumn of 1975, however, I was paying one of my regular calls on my uncle Harry Nelson at his bungalow in Melrose Road, Biggin Hill, when, having left the room, he returned carrying a heavy parcel which he placed on the table beside me. The loose brown paper wrapping fell slowly away to reveal a pile of about fifty old, and very dirty, 6½" x 4¾" glass photographic negatives. I cannot recall the exact words he used at the time but he said something to the effect that it was about time he handed down what remained of his father's photographic work to someone who would value and appreciate it.

That person was me, mainly because I happened to be the only other member of the Nelson family who had stayed on in Biggin Hill and had any affection for the place, but there was a little more to it than that. Harry Nelson, as well as having a great reputation as a prize winning vegetable grower, is a compulsive storyteller. On countless occasions, more often than not over a glass of 'Doctor Brown' or 'Captain Morgan', I had listened to his tales of old Biggin Hill and of the people and events which influenced its development since he first came here as a boy of seven in 1903. The negatives which he was handing to me would give substance to a great many of those stories.

Their survival makes an unusual story in itself. My grandfather, who had worked hard and profited little from his business, did not encourage any of his five children to take up photography, so that on his death in 1926 all his negatives were stored away in the loft of his bungalow in Melrose Road. There they remained undisturbed for twenty years in a wooden building within a few hundred yards of the end of the main runway of what was to become the busiest R.A.F. fighter station in the Battle of Britain. With my grandmother evacuated to the comparative safety of a flat in Westerham, the place was unoccupied and unlocked for long periods, but astonishingly, it escaped damage from the high explosive and incendiary bombs which so often fell in the area. A direct hit from any one of these would have spelt instant disaster.

When my grandmother died in 1945, arrangements were made for the bungalow to be sold and Uncle Harry, not wishing to abandon the fruits of his father's labour, conveyed the negatives across the road to his garden shed for safe keeping. There they stayed for the next thirty years, reasonably dry and protected, but lacking all the other care and attention which the experts recommend for the preservation of our photographic heritage.

Black-faced ghosts of the past stared out and strange, yet somehow familiar, buildings and landscapes could be seen when the negatives were held up to the light. I could not wait to find out who or what each one portrayed. In the event, it took a great deal longer than I had expected to perfect first how to clean and store and then how to produce actual photographs from these fragile records of the past. It was not until 17th October 1976 that I was able to watch the gradual appearance, in my developing tray, of the first of many photographs which had not seen the light of day at least since the death of my grandfather fifty years ago to the month.

I took my first efforts to show Uncle Harry. He was delighted to see them, and there was for me the added pleasure that they triggered off an abundance of new reminiscences. Often after that, during my visits, he would present me with a further batch of negatives all of which now form a unique archive of Biggin Hill and the surrounding area between 1903 and 1926.

In 1979 I was asked to give an informal village history talk to a meeting of a local organisation. Other invitations followed, and I was very soon struck by the keen interest shown by old and new residents alike in the village of bygone days. I hope that this book will sustain and widen that interest, and that as well as giving old-timers the incentive for a little nostalgia, it will provide newcomers to the village with an insight into Biggin Hill as it was in the first quarter of this century. It may also help to convince those with a feeling for local history that Biggin Hill is not just the name of a famous airfield, but a place which offers ample scope for historical enquiry and research.

I am deeply grateful to all the people, too numerous for me to name individually, who have helped to provide the information contained in the pages which follow. I must however record my very special indebtedness to my uncle, Harry Nelson, and also to Biggin Hill's most ardent historian, Mrs Winnie Paine. I have also to thank my wife without whose encouragement and practical assistance *Grandfather's Biggin Hill* would not have been possible.

JOHN NELSON

Biggin Hill, 1982

PREFACE TO THE 2ND EDITION

When I published the first edition of this book towards the end of 1982, it was warmly received by Biggin Hill people still living locally and by former residents who had moved away. That Christmas it was the most popular present in the village and over the holiday, when families met together, the book was the subject of discussion frequently leading to heated arguments, often as to the identities of people, or the names of houses, appearing in the photographs. I had countless telephone calls from people so pleased to find themselves in the pictures or to have been reminded of relations, friends and places as they knew them long ago. My wife, Stella, took a call from an elderly lady in Devon who said that her terminally ill husband had seen photos in the book that recalled for him happy past times in Biggin Hill and she was so grateful he was dying a contented man.

The last copies of the first edition of *Grandfather's Biggin Hill* were sold some years ago but on a number of occasions original purchasers have contacted me with the same story; that they would like to replace their copy because they had loaned it to a friend or neighbour and had never seen it again. All I have been able to suggest to them is that occasionally copies can be seen for sale on eBay or found on the shelves of secondhand bookshops.

I was therefore pleased to be approached, early in 2010, by Simon Finch, Local History Librarian at the Central Library, London Borough of Bromley, with a proposal that a second edition of *Grandfather's Biggin Hill* might be published by the Library as No 6 in their series of *Bromley Local Histories*. In agreeing to this proposal I have insisted that, even though the page size of the series is smaller, the whole of the contents of the first edition, text, photographs and captions must be reproduced.

A good deal has happened in Biggin Hill over the past twenty-eight years. Many of the old houses and other buildings, familiar to us all in 1982, have been demolished to make way for modern houses, blocks of flats, shops and offices. Businesses have closed down or moved away but more importantly in those years death has deprived us of so many of the old Biggin Hill people whose memories and recollections contributed so much to *Grandfather's*

Biggin Hill, among them my uncle Harry Nelson, Winnie Paine and Arthur Blake.

This new edition has provided an opportunity for me to make corrections, few, I am pleased to say, to the original text and captions. Notably the photographs of Temple's (**36-38**) have been placed in their correct sequence and **125** has been re-located. Elsewhere there have been amendments to reflect information which has come to light, and changes that have taken place, since 1982. Readers may identify others and are invited to advise the publishers in order that the book can be appropriately amended from time to time.

I very much hope that this second edition of *Grandfather's Biggin Hill* will be as successful a publication as the first and that it will provide newcomers with an insight into what has gone before, as well as going some way towards replacing those first editions which their purchasers loaned to friends and neighbours and never saw again!

JOHN NELSON

Biggin Hill, 2010

INTRODUCTION - 1982

BIGGIN HILL, in recent years, has been going through a period of intense change both in its appearance and character. Property development on a large scale has brought with it rapid growth in population, new and improved roads, shops, schools and firms of estate agents. What people are happy to go on calling a village is by certain standards a town of some size, but our new towns were properly planned, and many of our older ones grew up around what were originally villages centring on a main street, inn and parish church. Biggin Hill has had the advantages of neither a new nor an old town; it just started, almost in the middle of nowhere, and then it grew.

Ninety or so years ago, as a place on the map, Biggin Hill did not exist. Certainly there had been the ancient Biggin Hill Farm which occupied what were then fields on all sides of the Jail Lane and Main Road junction. The

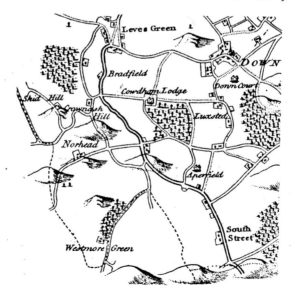

The Biggin Hill area as it appeared about 1800. (From a map published in Hasted's 'The History and Topographical Survey of the County of Kent')

unfenced area of land bordering on the road near the 'Black Horse', too, had been called Biggin Hill Green for several hundred years. What is now the widespread residential area of Biggin Hill, however, was almost entirely farmland forming part of the Manor of Aperfield in the parish of Cudham, Kent.

The name Aperfield in early times was spelt in a variety of different ways, one of the first recorded being Apuldrefield, almost certainly derived from what in modern English would be 'apple tree field'. A large field in which the houses of Aperfield Road and Village Green Avenue now stand was known more than three hundred years ago as 'Old Orchard' which tends to affirm this definition. It would seem, there is not as yet, an acceptable explanation for the origin of the name Biggin Hill, but there are several credible ones to choose from.

No pre-conquest references to the manor have been discovered, but it is recorded that Aperfield was one of the Manors which William the Conqueror presented to his half brother, Bishop Odo of Bayeux, following the victory of the Normans over King Harold in 1066. The Manor subsequently passed into the possession of a succession of eminent families including de Apuldrefield, de Foxle, Denny, Lennard (of Chevening), Dacre, Knowe, Bartholomew, Geary and Christy, although few of them actually resided there. It is not intended in this book, however, to attempt a detailed history of the Manor. For those who may wish to pursue it, this can be found in a work entitled *Some Account of the Manor of Apuldrefield in the Parish of Cudham, Kent*, by G. Steinman Steinman, F.S.A., and also in Hasted's *The History and Topographical Survey of the County of Kent*.

At the end of the seventeenth century, Aperfield was held by Thomas Lord Dacre, Earl of Sussex, who leased a very substantial part of it to Anne Brasier, a widow who died in 1726 and was buried in Cudham Church. In 1699 a survey of the manorial land leased to Mrs Brasier was carried out and a plan prepared, the outline of which bears a remarkable resemblance to Biggin Hill as it appears on maps today. The original plan, measuring 8' x 4', can still be inspected in the Kent County Archives Office at Maidstone, and its upper section is reproduced on page 14 by kind permission of the Archivist.

On 3rd June 1835, the Manor was sold by the then owner, Sir William Richard Powlett Geary, Bt., M.P., to John Christy of Hatcham Manor in New Cross. There was at that time an ancient manor house situated close to where the large cedar tree stands in Aperfield Road, but Steinman, who was the son-in-law of John Christy, says that the building, 'having long been occupied by farmers had become reduced to a very mean residence'. It was taken down and a new house, built on its site, was completed between 1835 and 1844.

Ownership remained in the hands of the Christy family for some sixty years, passing on the death of John, in the 1870s, to his son George. During that period arable farming and the rearing of livestock, in particular sheep, on the estate continued. At South Street Farm, Westerham Hill, also owned by the Christys, there was, by the early 1890s, a notable stud farm where a renowned and handsome hackney stallion named *Aperfield* was stabled.

In the *Bromley and District Times* of 7th June 1895 there appeared an announcement that Messrs. Baxter, Payne & Lepper, acting on behalf of the Executors of the Will of Mr. G. Christy, would sell by auction at The Mart, Tokenhouse Yard, London E.C., on Wednesday 3rd July 1895,

'...The Freehold Residential, Sporting and Agricultural Estate known as "Aperfield Court" comprising about 502a. 1r. 35p. of rich pasture, arable and woodland including a Family Residence standing in a miniature park, surrounded by pleasure grounds and the necessary glass houses, buildings, cottages, lodges &c...Portions of the estate must become valuable for building purposes, it possesses beautiful scenery, is well timbered, and affords many picturesque sites. The sporting is good, the land capital for stock rearing, and some of the Lots could not be excelled for poultry farming or horticulture...'

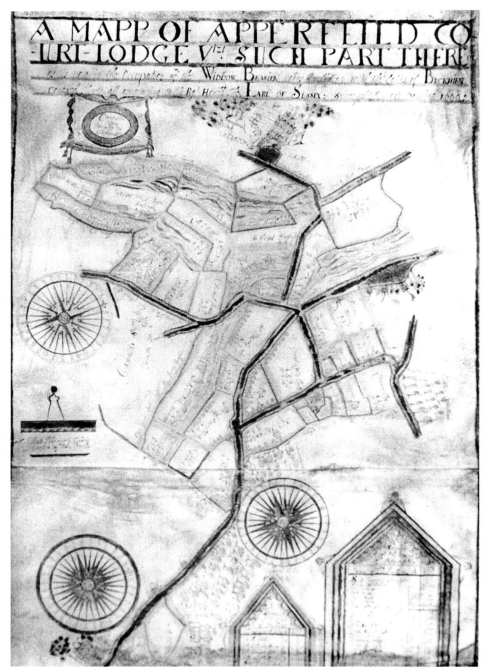

Upper section of the 1699 plan of Aperfield now in the care of the Kent County Archives office, Maidstone.

When the Manor of Aperfield was sold in July 1707 by the Earl of Sussex to Thomas Knowe of Downe, the consideration paid was £3,050. At the auction in July 1895, the estate, divided into sixteen lots, was sold for a total sum of £11,320, the highest price realised by any lot, probably Aperfield Court itself, being £2,800. The buyer of this and most of the agricultural land was Frederick Henry Dougal.

Mr. F. H. Dougal

Mr Dougal was no country gentleman. He lived at 148 Merton Road, Wandsworth, SW., maintaining an office at 62 (later 453) Strand, London WC, where he carried on business under the intriguing title of the Unclaimed Money Registry. It seems, however, that he owned some part of Biggin Hill Farm before the Aperfield auction, since there had been in April 1895, complaints to the Cudham Parish Council of him having unlawfully encroached on Biggin Hill Green.

Dougal had not the slightest intention to run Aperfield on the same lines as the Christys. His ideas were quite different. What he proposed to do was to divide the land into plots and sell them off quite cheaply to anyone who wished to buy them, and for whatever purpose, since the land at that time was not subject to any Building Regulations. Plans of the estate were drawn up, allocating a number to each plot, but *planning* in its present day sense was nowhere to be seen. The existing roads such as the Main Road, Stock Hill, Polesteeple Hill, Norheads Lane and Oaklands Lane were not realigned in any way. Hedges and fences which formed the boundaries of fields served as natural courses for new roads, it being necessary just to go to the expense of providing a parallel fence along the other side. Only in places where this procedure would not allow land to be divided into saleable plots on both sides were new roads constructed which did not conform to the traditional field layout. There were no kerbs or pavements, but trees such as horse chestnut, lime and poplar, planted at intervals along both sides of some roads, served to give a measure of protection to the footpath, as well as creating pleasant avenues.

Road construction itself involved a minimum of expenditure on materials. Flint and chalk were plentiful locally and, when spread on the surface and compressed by steamroller, produced a road adequate to stand up to the traffic of the time. Regular use by heavy vehicles in later years, however, progressively turned many of the new roads into deeply rutted tracks with long stretches of virtually impassable mud and deep puddles in all but the driest weather. Beyond any shadow of doubt, there was nothing which over the years caused greater discord and resentment in Biggin Hill than the deplorable state of the unmade roads.

As for the names by which the roads were called, some, such as Hillcrest, Highfield, Belvedere and The Grove alluded to their locations. The use of Royal christian names, such as Victoria, Edward, Alexandra and Arthur reflected the special affection enjoyed by the Queen and her family. Names for such as Melody, Melrose, Rosehill, and York Roads, Lebanon Gardens and East Hill were chosen by Mr. Dougal because they were thoroughfares which he knew well close to his home in Wandsworth.

The estate having been divided up into plots and reasonable access arranged, the marketing operation began and Mr. Dougal appointed as his official manager and estate agent Mr. Jesse Terry, who lived in one of the old thatched cottages which stood on the land fronting on to Biggin Hill Green, now occupied by Lunar Close. Large hoardings were erected and a brochure full of recommendations from satisfied early purchasers was produced and distributed widely extolling the advantages of acquiring land in Biggin Hill. It was Dougal himself who decided to apply this name to the areas he was selling off, retaining the name Aperfield for the land to the eastern side of the Main Road between North and South Lodges on which Aperfield Court stood, and which had yet to be placed on the market.

According to the brochure there was beautiful scenery everywhere and opportunities for business ventures of many kinds were waiting to be seized. Who, in due course could fail to make a handsome profit when plots with a twenty foot frontage could be bought for as little as £10, with immediate possession on the payment of a deposit of £1, the balance being due in half-yearly instalments of ten shillings (50p) over 9 years at 5% interest?

A press advertising campaign was launched, with maps showing which plots were still unsold and a small fleet of Daimler passenger vehicles, acquired by Dougal, plied between Bromley Post Office and The Mill House, Biggin Hill. There were three journeys a day in each direction, and the fare was one shilling (5p).

Mr. Dougal and Mr. Terry were available, by appointment, to accompany prospective purchasers to view land on any part of the Estate, and regular auction sales 'preceded by luncheon' were conducted by Mr Terry in the Auction Room on the heights of Mount Pleasant. One further attraction was the coming of the railway. A feature of the Estate Map was the line of the Orpington and Tatsfield Light Railway which was to cross the Main Road with a station about half-way between St. Winifred's and Belvedere Roads. Like some of Mr Dougal's other visions, however, it failed to materialise.

A considerable number of plots were sold and although houses and bungalows for permanent occupation were built, people were, for the most part, in no hurry to settle on the estate. The majority chose just to visit their land for picnics on summer weekends and bank holidays. A modest building was then found useful in which to keep the deckchairs and garden shears and to provide cover during the occasional shower. Gradually the landscape became interspersed with summer houses, sheds and temporary buildings of all shapes, colours and sizes. There was no limit to the ingenuity of people in what they placed on their land to provide shelter, including old railway carriages, tram cars, caravans and the bodies of derelict lorries.

Some houses, principally those built around the turn of the century, were of brick with slate or tiled roofs and a few of these remain, including 'Blandford Villa' in Arthur Road, 'Whitecliff' in Sutherland Avenue, 'The Haven' (now 172) and 'Highclere' (now 184) in the Main Road and Mount Pleasant Cottages [1]. To get to Biggin Hill, however, meant an uphill journey, over poorly maintained roads, from whichever direction one came and the transport of heavy building materials was an expensive matter for the kind of people who were only able to buy land locally because it was cheap. Thus lighter materials such as breeze blocks, wood, corrugated iron and asbestos sheets were more greatly favoured by the early twentieth century arrivals.

Several local firms opened up to erect buildings to any purchaser's requirements, and it must be said that some of the work carried out by these firms was to a very high standard. Some (but by no means all) of the bungalows which were in later years indiscriminately described as 'wooden shacks' incorporated first class carpentry and joinery craftsmanship and materials of excellent quality.

A strong community spirit soon began to emerge among the permanent residents of Biggin Hill, but to begin with there was no public hall which could be used as a focal point for their activities.

The first hall to serve as a meeting place for use on social occasions came early in 1903 when The Beacon Concert Hall was opened by Mr. Francis J. Vant, proprietor of The Beacon Refreshment Rooms. It measured thirty feet by fifty feet and was built well back towards Sutherland Avenue on land to the rear of what is now 156 Main Road (Furlongs)[2]. The hall fell into disuse in the late 1930's, but as a wartime drill hall for the Home Guard, it again proved its usefulness. Soon after the war, just as it was being converted into a cinema, the hall caught fire late one evening and in no time burned to the ground.

A public meeting, the first to be held in 'Mr Vant's New Room', took place on 27th February 1903, presided over by the Vicar of Cudham, the Rev. H.A. Curtis; its purpose was 'to consider whether some further provision

1. All bar 'Whitecliff' and Mount Pleasant Cottages were gone by 2010.
2. By 2010 this had become the Nat West Bank and renumbered 158.

Aperfield Court Estate

BIGGIN HILL,

Westerham Road, CUDHAM, KENT.

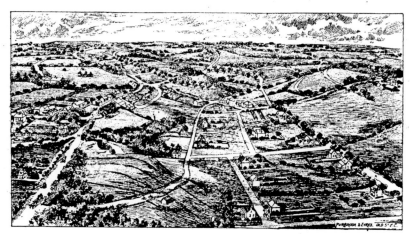

250 PLOTS OF VALUABLE

FREEHOLD BUILDING LAND

Will be sold by Auction, on the Estate, on

EASTER MONDAY, APRIL 8th, 1901,

AT **2** O'CLOCK—PRECEDED BY LUNCHEON.

A Pleasant Drive from Bromley and Bicycle Ride from London, only 17 miles. Conveyances at Hayes Station to take intending Purchasers to Estate.

For Particulars and Plan apply ———

F. H. DOUGAL, 62, Strand, W.C.;

Or the Auctioneer—

J. TERRY, Biggin Hill, Cudham, Kent.

Handbill publicising an auction, on 8th April 1901, of land on the Aperfield Court Estate

could be made for the spiritual needs of Biggin Hill'. Clearly, the long walk to Cudham Church each Sunday was too much for all but the most robust of the faithful. Illness prevented the attendance of Mr Dougal, but a letter from him was read, offering to donate a site for a mission church at the corner of the Main Road and Polesteeple Hill (now Temple Road), together with the sum of £25 towards building costs. Mr. A.C. Norman the owner of Norheads, agreed to contribute a similar sum and there were various other promises of financial support. A committee was formed and a resolution passed to the effect that a mission church should be erected in Biggin Hill.

Within less than a year, the Church of St. Mark was built on the site given by Mr. Dougal at a cost of £230, and a service of dedication by the Lord Bishop of Dover took place in the church on 21st January 1904. The Church was described at the time as a temporary iron structure and that, whenever the district had sufficiently developed, it was intended to erect a permanent brick or stone building. The temporary church, in fact, remained in use for the next fifty-five years. The collection at the dedication service, amounting to £5 4s. 2$^1/_2$d., was applied towards the building expenses and the Rev. T. Gwynne Davies was appointed the first Curate-in-Charge. He did not, however, stay long, in common with most of the other Curates in the early days of St. Mark's.

Early on the morning of Wednesday, 13th July 1904, Mr. F.H. Dougal was found dead in his bed at 148 Merton Road, Wandsworth. He had been ailing for some time, having suffered from heart disease and dropsy, and he had been greatly affected by the loss of his wife some six months previously. His death, however, at the early age of fifty-four, came as a considerable shock. Only the week before, he had been at Aperfield attending to prospective purchasers, and had been in quite good spirits. His funeral was at Wandsworth Cemetery on 15th July and those present included the Rev. H.A. Curtis, Vicar of Cudham, Mr. Freeman who was one of the executors, Jesse Terry, Francis Vant and Mr. D.B. Milbank.

Clearly Dougal had been something of an autocrat and the successful start to the marketing of the Aperfield Court Estate had been largely attributable to his own personality and enthusiasm. There was no way in which he could be replaced by executors and trustees obliged to act on the cautious advice of solicitors. The impetus was gone, and within a short while the Daimler passenger service had been withdrawn. Jesse Terry continued to act as agent for the executors but by now he was sixty and no doubt beginning to find climbing the hills all around him more than he could manage. Before long, Mr. D.B. Milbank, who had moved into 'The Mill House' began to undertake some of the duties of the managing agent and together they carried on for the trustees the enterprise which Dougal had initiated.

It was well after the First World War before the trustees offered for sale the land to the east of the Main Road, opening up Allenby and Haig Roads, named after two of the great soldiers of the War. Restrictive covenants were, however, placed on this land which had not been imposed elsewhere on the Estate. One of these required that no trade, business or manufacture should be carried out on any plot. Thus the village was saddled with having a main thoroughfare with all its shops strung out along one side and none on the other.

For years Biggin Hill never really prospered; it was an embarrassment and a problem so far as the centres of local government in Bromley and Orpington were concerned, and yet there was never stagnation nor lack of support for local tradesmen or for a wide variety of village organisations and activities. Frederick Henry Dougal's predictions about the profits to be made from investment in his land eventually came true as well, but not until long after most of the original purchasers had ceased to care.

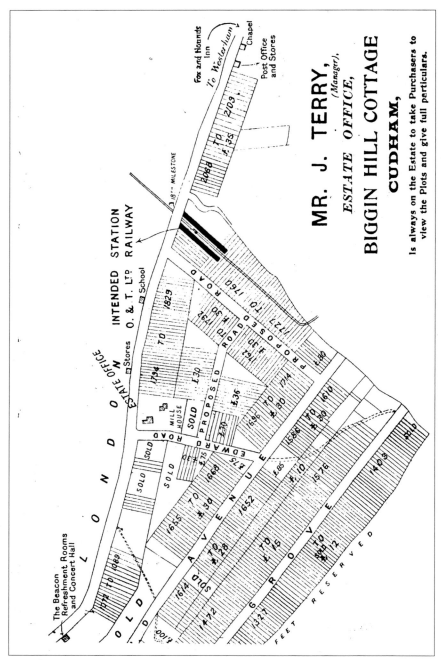

Part of a map prepared in 1903 showing the division into plots of the southern section of the Aperfield Court Estate and the position of the intended railway station.

William Henry Nelson

MY GRANDFATHER was the eldest of eight children of Alfred Horatio Nelson, an artist who took up professional photography work in its pioneering days and built up at Sherland Works in Twickenham an important international business in the manufacture and supply of photographic chemicals, dry plates and equipment. As a young man, my grandfather worked in the family firm, but by the early 1890s, he had become almost exclusively preoccupied with the running of his own photographic business and studio in King Street, Twickenham. It would appear however, that, with increasing competition, business became very difficult and he was obliged to close down for a year or so while he went to work in Ireland. He returned to Twickenham to try again with a studio at St. Margaret's, but it was an uphill struggle.

How my grandfather came to hear of the Aperfield Court Estate we will never know. Perhaps his brother-in-law, James Newberry, a builder whose yard was at West Street in Bromley, had told him about the motor-buses he had seen bearing the enticing message '£10 PLOTS'. With a wife and family to be maintained the prospects offered by a new life in the country at Biggin Hill in an expanding community were too great to be ignored.

Early in 1903, a preliminary reconnoitre took place, and plot 21, priced at £30, was decided upon in Melrose Road, where there was at least a supply of mains water, if not any gas or electricity. The next thing was to provide a roof over the family's head, so the basic materials for a timber bungalow were purchased and sent by rail to Hayes Station. At Hayes, my grandfather negotiated with the contractor, Mr Price, for the delivery of the materials by two horse-drawn wagons to the site at Biggin Hill. On arrival at the 'Black Horse', however, the drivers, learning that they were required to go down Stock Hill into the valley, insisted on an extra 'danger money' payment. They were eventually given a meal and some liquid refreshment in the bar close by, thereby averting their threat to deposit both loads on Biggin Hill Green.

My grandmother duly arrived with her children and all the family furniture and possessions. Temporary accommodation was obtained in Vale Cottages, one of which cottages remains today, close to the roundabout at the foot of Stock Hill. Without any previous building experience, my grandfather set about erecting 'Trafalgar Bungalow', sometimes known as 'The Victory' at the corner of Melrose Road and Arthur Road, opposite to the plots where his son Harry was to build his own bungalow some years later. From there, for the next twenty-three years, he carried on his photographic business. Lack of artificial light was a problem, but supplies of gas and electricity did not arrive during his lifetime. The oil lamps which were used to light the bungalow were of little use to a photographer and most of his camera work and printing of photographs in wooden frames using *printing-out paper* was done in natural light.

Trade to begin with was slow, but grandmother, an accomplished musician, gave piano lessons to help balance the family budget. There were not as many people around to have their photographs taken as he had hoped, so W.H. Nelson saw that the best way of making a living was by means of picture postcards.

Over the years he took many photographs of Biggin Hill and places nearby for this purpose and produced thousands of cards which he himself sold and which could be obtained through shops and Post Offices in the district. With his camera strapped to his tricycle he would ride round photographing any view which he felt might appeal to the postcard buyer. Postcards were his bread and butter, but as Biggin Hill grew and the community developed, so did the variety of work he was able to undertake.

I have selected for this book one hundred and fifty W.H. Nelson photographs of Biggin Hill (including Westerham Hill) its landscape, buildings, people and events. These have been arranged as near as possible by location, beginning with Aperfield Court and its surroundings, followed by a progression along the Main Road from the R.A.F. Main Gate to South Street Baptist Chapel and to several other points on the higher ground. Starting from Stock Hill there is then an anti-clockwise tour around the valley and, to conclude, a miscellany of people, groups and events.

I hope that individually many of the photographs will provide pleasure and interest and that together they will re-create the scene and atmosphere that was grandfather's Biggin Hill.

ESTABLISHED OVER 20 YEARS.

W. H. NELSON,

Portrait and Landscape Photographer,

Enlargements, Framing, etc.

MELROSE ROAD, BIGGIN HILL, KENT.

W. H. Nelson's advertisement in the Cudham Parish Magazine, 1925.

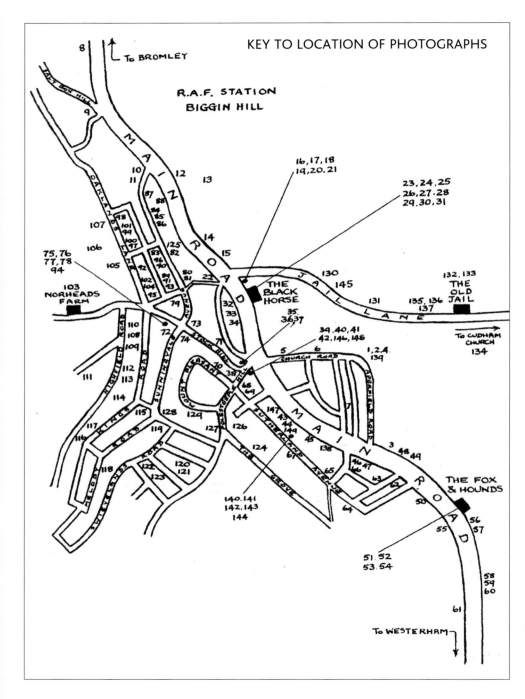

KEY TO LOCATION OF PHOTOGRAPHS

1. APERFIELD COURT

$\mathcal{A}$n ancient manor house which stood for several centuries close to the large cedar tree in Aperfield Road was demolished shortly after the estate was purchased in 1835 by John Christy. At that time the remains of a moat could still be seen, indicating that it had, in former times, been a place of some importance. The last manor house, part of which is seen in this photograph, was built on the same site between 1835 and 1844 and was itself taken down, together with its stables, outbuildings and oast-house soon after the First World War.

2. THE CEDAR TREE, APERFIELD ROAD

*T*here is a popular belief that the cedar tree was planted after having been brought back from the Crusades in the 12th century by Sir Henry de Apuldrefield, the Lord of the Manor, who, with his son Henry, is recorded as having served under Richard I at Acre in 1191. Some experts, however, say that the cedar is unlikely to be much more than 250 years old. Aperfield Road, constructed in the early 1920s passes close to the tree. The corner of Aperfield Court can be seen on the far left of the photograph.

3. SOUTH LODGE, MAIN ROAD

*A*bout the time of the 1835-44 rebuilding by John Christy, a new southern approach road to Aperfield Court was constructed, with a pair of tall iron entrance gates on the Main Road about fifty yards to the Westerham side of the present junction with Aperfield Road. At this entrance was built the South Lodge, which is still standing today, although considerably modernised. In this picture the manor house can be seen in the distance between the lodge and gates.

4. ARTILLERYMEN IN THE YARD OF APERFIELD COURT

$\mathcal{I}$n the 1914-18 War, Aperfield Court was taken over for military use and here we see mounted artillerymen and a gun carriage in the yard of the manor house. During the latter part of the War and for some time afterwards the house was used as an out-station for wireless experiments by the Instrument Design Establishment of the R.A.F. By 1922 the land on which the house had stood was being offered for sale as building plots.

5. APERFIELD COURT ESTATE

$\mathcal{H}$ere hay-making is in progress on the Aperfield Court Estate about 1918. The photograph appears to have been taken in the south-east corner of the Recreation Ground with the trees surrounding the Spitfire Youth Centre to the right. The West Cudham Recreation Ground, as it was previously known, was purchased by the Council, together with the land for the cemetery and allotments, from the Aperfield Court Estate Trustees in 1930 for £1,600 and a further £1,900 was spent on landscaping, fencing and improvements.

6. POND, CHURCH ROAD

*B*efore the days of proper drainage, the simplest way to dispose of surface water was to channel it off into ponds, of which there were several in Biggin Hill. The old pond shown here is marked on the Aperfield Map of 1699, but in recent years it was drained and filled in. It is now the site of the Spitfire Youth Centre in Church Road.

7. POND, VILLAGE GREEN WAY

$\mathcal{B}$oth this pond and most of Village Green Way itself are now lost amongst the properties built between Village Green Avenue and Allenby Road. The reflection of the cow in the water is one of the few examples where W. H. Nelson has introduced a touch of photographic art into his work, which was almost invariably unpretentious and matter of fact.

8. 'FORGE COTTAGES', MAIN ROAD

*A*t the point where Hanbury Drive meets the Main Road, near to the R.A.F. Station Main Gate, there is today a triangular area of grass and it is here that these cottages stood. The guy-ropes of a radio mast to the right of the picture indicate a date about 1917. Dutch elm disease eventually killed the large tree in the centre of the picture and it was felled on 29th October 1976.

9. 'CROWN ASH COTTAGE', SALT BOX HILL

*T*his cottage, which still stands at the junction of Crown Ash and Salt Box Hills, looks much as it did about a century ago, although the ivy or creeper on the front elevation has been removed. There has also been some considerable improvement in the condition of the road surface since the photograph was taken.

Sunningvale Avenue
Biggin Hill

10. SUNNINGVALE AVENUE

*A*t Sunningvale Avenue travellers along the Main Road from Leaves Green caught their first glimpse through the trees of the valley section of the Aperfield Court Estate. Just off to the left of the picture was a tea garden called Kosi Korner, later renamed Sunningvale Tea Rooms.

11. THE VALLEY FROM SUNNINGVALE AVENUE

A few yards below the trees in the last photograph this view right along the valley opened up, looking over Arthur Road, Kings Road and up to Swievelands. From the view here, seen as it was about 1904, it is not difficult to imagine that only a few years previously this had all been farming land.

12. CORNER BY THE ENTRANCE TO 'KOONOWLA', MAIN ROAD

One would never suspect that this was once the view along what is now the start of a section of dual carriageway road looking in the Bromley direction. The white gates on the right, leading to a house called 'Koonowla', are roughly in line with the present entrance to Biggin Hill Airport Trading Estate.

13. CHILDREN AND STAFF AT KOONOWLA CONVALESCENT HOME

Situated by the side of the present approach road to Biggin Hill Airport Trading Estate, 'Koonowla' was bequeathed about 1910 to the Victoria Hospital for Sick Children for use as a convalescent home. When the Royal Flying Corps arrived in December 1916, the house was requisitioned as an Officers Mess, and the children and nursing staff moved out, never to return. No trace of 'Koonowla' now remains, but its name has been perpetuated in Koonowla Close on the small modern housing estate just off Jail Lane.

14. MAIN ROAD, APPROACHING THE 'BLACK HORSE'

*T*his stretch of road is still just recognisable, although now considerably widened and with pavements on both sides. The land to the right falls away sharply into the valley so that the road widening necessitated the removal of the trees and the excavation of several feet of the bank on the left.

15. THE 'NIGHTINGALE' TEA GARDENS, MAIN ROAD

*O*f the many tea gardens which, between the Wars, were spaced out along the Main Road, the 'Nightingale' was one which survived longer than most. The hedge and driveway have been replaced by a wide concrete forecourt and the premises, much extended, are now occupied by a firm of timber merchants. It is believed that part of the premises was at one time an outbuilding of Biggin Hill Farm.

16. OLD SURREY FOXHOUNDS MEET AT BIGGIN HILL GREEN, 1906

*J*n one of the few dated photographs by W. H. Nelson, we see huntsmen and hounds on the green opposite the 'Black Horse' preparing to move off on a fox hunt. Most of the trees in the picture have now gone and road widening at this point has severely reduced the width of the Green.

17. BIGGIN HILL GREEN

The unfenced areas of land on both sides of the Main Road at the junction with Jail Lane have been known as Biggin Hill Green for several hundred years. 'Biggin Hill House' to the right of this picture, which adjoins the Green, was purchased in 1904 by Mr. W. F. Foster, who said, some years later, that at that time there was no such place as Biggin Hill and the locality had taken its name from his house. The cattle trough and drinking fountain, now planted with flowers, which today stands at the edge of the Green, was installed in 1923.

18. MR. WILLIAM F. FOSTER

*A*fter the 1914-18 War it was agreed that Cudham Parish should have a War Memorial to the fallen and that the best place for this to be erected was on Biggin Hill Green. Mr. Foster, a solicitor and member of the Cudham Parish Council, offered to donate the Green for this purpose, after fencing off a portion of it adjoining 'Biggin Hill House' for his own use. There was strong local opinion that it was not his to give and one night the fence he had erected was broken down by unknown hands. After much acrimony the 'deeds' were handed over to the Parish at a public meeting on 16th September 1922.

19. UNVEILING THE WAR MEMORIAL (1)

The unveiling was performed by Group Captain Blandy, D.S.O., a former Station Commander at R.A.F. Biggin Hill, at a ceremony held on 21st March 1923. This picture shows the scene at the commencement of the proceedings. Contingents from the R.A.F., Royal Field Artillery, Royal Engineers and the School of Signalling formed the Guard of Honour.

20. UNVEILING THE WAR MEMORIAL (2)

$\mathcal{I}$n the presence of a large gathering of local ex-servicemen, residents and schoolchildren the ceremony began with a brief service conducted by Ministers from St. Mark's Aperfield and Cudham Baptist Church. This photograph was taken after the unveiling had been carried out, with the rifles of the Guard of Honour 'at the present' during the sounding of the 'Last Post'.

21. UNVEILING THE WAR MEMORIAL (3).

Wreaths have now been laid and the Memorial dedicated by the Vicar of Cudham, the Rev. Bryan O'Loughlin. Here 'Reveille' is being sounded before the singing of the National Anthem. The memorial, of granite, was made by Francis Chappell & Sons of Bromley and beneath it is a brick structure in which were placed small quantities of earth collected from the gardens of each of the thirty-two servicemen who died.

22. MR. JESSE TERRY, ESTATE AGENT

*T*he first official agent for the Aperfield Court Estate was Mr. Terry who lived first in one of the thatched cottages on Biggin Hill Green, and later at 'Hogarth', Polesteeple Hill. He is seen here outside his estate office, which was situated on the opposite side of the Green to the 'Black Horse', a reminder that Biggin Hill's estate agents have not always operated from prestigious premises. Mr. Terry died at Christmas 1926.

23. BIGGIN HILL COTTAGES AND THE 'BLACK HORSE'

*P*erhaps more than any other, this picture captures the atmosphere of Biggin Hill at the turn of the last century. The old thatched cottages, formerly belonging to Biggin Hill Farm, were built on the land now occupied by Lunar Close. With all those hoardings in Mr. Terry's front garden, what passer-by could fail to observe that there was cheap land for sale in the district?

24. THE OLD 'BLACK HORSE' (1)

$\mathcal{T}$his old postcard shows how the curiosity of bystanders used to be aroused by a photographer at work. The old 'Black Horse', although formerly a pair of cottages, had been a public-house for many years. In the centre of the picture, with his dog, is Mr. Charles Harris, a traveller for the Bromley ironmongery firm of J. Morton Crouch. It was he who supplied the corrugated iron for the roof of W. H. Nelson's bungalow at 2s. 9d. a sheet.

25. THE OLD 'BLACK HORSE' (2)

$\mathcal{T}$he year is about 1906 and the long shadows indicate that it is early morning with the horse bus about to begin the day's work. The old 'Black Horse' was then nearing the end of its life, being demolished in 1908 and much of the rubble used to fill up an old pond on the Green.

26. THE BROMLEY HORSE BUS

*L*ocal horse-bus services during the early part of the century were provided by Mr. F. Capon whose main stables were at Crow Hill, Downe. The vehicle here, which was built by G. Osgood of High Road, Pratts Bottom, Chelsfield, is being driven by Bill Salmon of Hillcrest Road, whose son Jack is the boy beside him. There were three services a day between the 'Black Horse', Biggin Hill and 'The Rising Sun', Bromley, via Hayes, with changes of horse at 'The Fox', Keston.

27. THE ORPINGTON HORSE BUS (WINTER)

*H*ot breath rises in front of the horses and frost obscures the windows of the bus waiting outside the 'Black Horse' on a cold winter morning. This vehicle ran on another of Mr. Capon's routes via Jail Lane, Downe, Farnborough Village and Tubbenden Lane to Orpington Station.

28. THE ORPINGTON BUS (SUMMER)

$\mathcal{I}$n contrast to the last picture, here we have a Capon bus at the same place on a warm summer's day. An open carriage with a canopy provides the service between Biggin Hill and Orpington Station.

29. THE FIRST MOTOR BUS LEAVING BIGGIN HILL

On 25th September 1913 the London General Omnibus Company started the first regular motor bus route through Biggin Hill. Numbered 95, the service ran between Bromley and Westerham Hill, via Keston Mark, the fare over the whole distance being 6d. (2½p). Here we see the first bus to run, pausing at Biggin Hill on the return journey to Bromley. On the upper deck local dignitaries pose for the photograph, with the estate agent, Mr. D. B. Milbank, centre right. On the lower deck, Professor Lambert stands by the conductor.

30. THE NEW 'BLACK HORSE'

*A*fter the demolition of the old building in 1908 the new 'Black Horse' was built on the same site and still appears much as it did over a hundred years ago. It was a Nalder & Collyer house from 1880 to around 1950 and in the photograph draymen from the brewery at Croydon are making a delivery. Note how the thatched cottages to the left have fallen into disrepair.

31. MOTOR VEHICLES AT THE 'BLACK HORSE'

*B*oth vehicles are Model 'T' Fords of around 1914. At the wheel of the car on the left is Harry Armstead, landlord of the 'Black Horse'; the boy and girl are his children. Despite the advertisement on the side, the one on the right was a service van belonging to the London General Omnibus Company.

SAUNDERS TEA GARDENS

BigginHill

32. SAUNDERS' TEA GARDENS

*I*n 1895, William Saunders moved from Croydon to commence business as a dairyman at 'Oak Cottage', Main Road, and later traded under the name of Biggin Hill Dairy. The land at the side of 'Oak Cottage', which can still be seen opposite Bramis House, soon joined the growing number of tea gardens and cyclist's rests. The photograph is taken looking back towards the Main Road, with 'Oak Cottage' on the right.

33. BIGGIN HILL STORES, MAIN ROAD

One of the first general stores in Biggin Hill was at 'Rose Cottage', which adjoined the premises of Mr. Saunders, opened in 1897 by Mrs. Harriet Chitty, who had formerly been at Skid Hill Farm. The business continued in the Chitty and Wicking families until the mid-1950s. The bill-head of Mrs. Harriet Chitty is reproduced below.

BIGGIN HILL STORES.

.... 190

M ....

Dr. to H. CHITTY,

Grocer, Cheesemonger, Oilman,

HARDWARE AND GENERAL STORES.

FAMILIES SUPPLIED.

34. BIGGIN HILL FORGE

$\mathcal{T}$he forge, which closed down about 1944, stood close to the Main Road at the corner of the land now occupied by the Automatic Telephone Exchange. Here we see the owner and blacksmith, Mr. John ('Jack') Tremain behind the anvil, with his striker, Bill Beadle, on the left. The 'Black Horse' can be seen in the distance and to the immediate right of the forge is a side view of one Baxter, Payne & Lepper's property advertising boards.

35. VIEW OF THE VALLEY FROM HILLCREST ROAD

$\mathcal{T}$his early photograph of the valley was taken about 1904 from where Temple's Stores later stood, at what is now the junction of Temple Road and Hillcrest Road. The view is over the former fields known as Little Stock and Great Stock from which Stock Hill received its name.

36. TEMPLE'S STORES (1)

Temple's opened their first store in Biggin Hill about 1908 on the corner of Hillcrest Road and the part of Polesteeple Hill now known as Temple Road, a site they were to occupy for the next sixty years. It was in a prime position to attract custom as it had to be passed by the majority of people proceeding to and from the valley by way of both Stock Hill and Polesteeple Hill.

37. TEMPLE'S STORES (2)

𝒯his was Temple's in 1914 after the business had grown and the premises had been improved and extended, but the Temple family's large house on the left and the shop were later destroyed in a disastrous fire.

Whatever the want ————

You can get it at

Temple's Ltd.

The Aperfield Stores

BIGGIN HILL, KENT

38. TEMPLE'S STORES (3)

*F*ollowing the fire in which Temple's shop was totally destroyed; business was carried on, until rebuilding was completed, in temporary premises shown here on the corner of Stock Hill and Polesteeple Hill below Mount Pleasant Cottages. The proprietor, Mr Thomas Temple, standing on the left, served on the Cudham Parish Council between 1919 and 1934 and was its Chairman from 1927. Although the shop was rebuilt in similar style, the house was replaced by a bungalow called 'Marne', but in the late 1960s, after the business had closed down, both bungalow and shop were demolished to make way for housing development.

39. ST. MARK'S CHURCH, APERFIELD (1)

When the Aperfield Court Estate was opened up, it soon became evident that, with the Parish Church of Cudham situated in the remotest corner of the parish, a 'chapel of ease' in Biggin Hill would be required. The temporary building, of timber construction clad in corrugated iron, was erected in 1903 and served the district until the new St. Mark's was consecrated in April 1959.

40. ST. MARK'S CHURCH, APERFIELD (2).

*I*n May 1904 it was announced in the *Cudham Parish Magazine* that Mr. Tothill of 'Koonowla' had accepted the office of Honorary Gardener to St. Mark's, adding '... his duties are to take care of the trees, shrubs and flowers, also he has the privilege of providing the necessary materials at his own expense'. As can be seen from this later photograph, the trees flourished and very soon obscured the view of the Church from the road.

41. ST. MARK'S CHURCH, INTERIOR

*L*it in its early days by oil lamps, the church seated about seventy people in individual chairs. The inside was lined with varnished match-boarding and heating was by means of a large round coke stove by the door at the rear. Close to the font, at the end of the centre aisle, was the rope which operated a single bell hung in a small spire. To the left of the altar was the organ and to the right, a door leading to the vestry.

42. MAIN ROAD NEAR ST. MARK'S CHURCH

$\mathcal{F}$rom a point on the pavement outside the Memorial Library, looking to the left, it is possible to observe the changes which have taken place at this spot after about a hundred years. To the right is St. Mark's Church and, on the far left, the shops which still stand at the corner of Lebanon Gardens.

43. MAIN ROAD AND 'THE BEACON'

$\mathcal{T}$his photograph of a scene unrecognisable today, was taken from the present Main Road junction with Haig Road looking towards Bromley. The building in the centre was 'The Beacon' Refreshment Rooms, owned by Mr. Francis Vant, who, in 1903, built the Beacon Concert Hall. Mr Allchin took over 'The Beacon' as a domestic stores in 1912. The field on the left behind the double white gate is now occupied by a small parade of shops.

44. THE CENTRAL HALL

$\mathcal{T}$he Biggin Hill Baptist Church was built in 1923, with considerable assistance from voluntary labour, to replace the old Chapel in Jail Lane. This photograph was taken at the site on 7th July 1923 on the occasion of 'Our Day' to raise money for the Building Fund. The speaker on the platform is Rev. H. M. Woodward, Curate-in-Charge at St. Mark's Church, lending support to a fellow Christian enterprise. In the background is the bungalow called 'Charlton' which was for many years the residence of Biggin Hill's district nurse.

45. 'HIGHCLERE', MAIN ROAD

*P*robably the most stately of the older Biggin Hill buildings was 'Highclere' now demolished and its site occupied by shops and offices. In later years a bottle collectors' and metal detector centre, it was for many years the celebrated 'Tea Pot', a popular venue for thousands of cyclists in the days when cycling was a major weekend sport. The large red teapot, mounted on a tall framework outside, was a well known landmark as well as being a coveted 'trophy' among locally based R.A.F. and Army units.

46. 'THE MILL HOUSE', MAIN ROAD

*T*here had been, for very many years, a working windmill called 'Pimlico Mill' on the land at the corner of Edward Road and the Main Road but this had fallen into disrepair and was dismantled about 1885. The timber structure on the far left of the picture is in the position where the mill originally stood. It would appear to have been erected, using recovered materials from the body of the mill, over parts of its lower section which were still in place when the photo was taken about 1908. No evidence of the mill now remains.

47. MR D. B. ('DAN') MILBANK

$\mathcal{M}$r. Milbank, who resided at 'The Mill House' from about 1907, eventually succeeded Jesse Terry as principal agent to the Trustees of the Aperfield Court Estate. Purchasers of land were obliged to attend on the ground with him to stake out the boundaries and contracts required that 'all measurements must be approved by Mr. Milbank before any boundary fences are erected'. Mr. Milbank died in 1926.

48. MAIN ROAD AT SOUTH LODGE

$\mathscr{A}$ny two ladies who risked walking along the Main Road in this position today would very soon be among the road accident statistics. South Lodge, with the pillars at the entrance gate to Aperfield Court, is on the left and beyond it, 'Coronation Terrace'.

49. 'CORONATION TERRACE', MAIN ROAD

*A*t a point about fifty yards behind where W. H. Nelson placed his camera for this photograph, it was planned that the (never-to-come) Orpington and Tatsfield Light Railway would cross the Main Road and Biggin Hill Station would be built. On the right, behind 'The Garth' and 'The Limes' is 'Coronation Terrace', erected in 1902 and said to have been planned as residences for the railway staff.

50. *'HAWTHORN COTTAGE', WESTERHAM HILL*

*L*ater called 'Rosemary', this was one of several old knapped flint cottages built on small-holdings in the district and dating back to the early nineteenth century. This cottage has been altered and modernised and is no longer visible behind a high fence and conifer trees.

51. OLD SURREY FOXHOUNDS AT THE 'FOX AND HOUNDS'

*I*t is a long time since a hunt has been seen in Biggin Hill, but in the early part of the last century hunting was a regular activity in the area. The 'meet' usually took place on the forecourt of a public-house, in this case the 'Fox and Hounds' at Westerham Hill and there was often a following of local people several hundred strong. The old motor-cycle in the foreground is an interesting model which has defied identification by the experts.

52. 'B' TYPE L.G.O.C. BUS No 95 AT THE 'FOX AND HOUNDS'

*T*he driver and conductor from Old Kent Road Garage pose proudly beside their bus parked at its terminus on the forecourt of the 'Fox and Hounds'. On the side is an announcement of an event which took place on 1st December 1913, so the picture was probably taken soon after that date. The products advertised inside the lower deck include *Pink's Jams and Marmalade, Jeyes Fluid, Bird's Custard and Phosferine Tonic.*

53. 'B' TYPE L.G.O.C. BUS No 136 AT THE 'FOX AND HOUNDS'

$\mathcal{L}$.G.O.C. route 95 ran for some six months before the number was changed to 136 on 30th March 1914. Here we see a 136 at the terminus, taken in the early summer of 1914, the bus coming from the garage at Catford (Code AN on the side) which was requisitioned soon after the outbreak of the First World War. At the right hand edge of the photograph the very back end of a gypsy caravan can be seen with a water container hanging on the tail-board.

.54. EAST SURREY TRACTION CO. LTD., 'P.S' TYPE No. s10 AT THE 'FOX AND HOUNDS'

$\mathcal{U}$nder an agreement with L.G.O.C., East Surrey started the s10 service between Bromley North and Reigate on 3rd June 1922, the fare for the whole journey being 2s. 6d. (12½p). This bus, PD 1366, came into service on 30th June 1924 and since, on 1st December 1924, the Metropolitan Police directed that the number be changed from s10 to 410, the picture was taken between those two dates. Note that solid tyres are still in use and remained so in this area until 1928. At about the same time the maximum permitted speed of buses with pneumatic tyres was increased from 12 to 20 m.p.h. The weighing machine in the background brings back memories, also the inevitable sign pointing to the tea gardens, a mandatory feature of a country pub at that time.

55. HALL'S STORES, WESTERHAM HILL

*T*he Hall family were in business at Westerham Hill for many years being pig farmers, carriers and fuel merchants as well as running this little general stores. Goods, advertisements and notices fill up every available space and observe, on the right, that they stored 'Motors, Horses and Traps'; not just the common bicycle as in the picture which follows.

56. TEA ROOMS AT WESTERHAM HILL

$\mathcal{A}$ popular day out for South Londoners was to cycle the uphill journey to Westerham Hill during the morning and to store their bicycles at one of the places where notices like the one above the double gate in this picture were displayed. After refreshment at one of the tea gardens and a walk in the country along any of the footpaths which converge at this point, the return journey in the evening was, for the most part, a pleasant downhill ride.

57. SOUTH STREET, WESTERHAM HILL

$\mathcal{S}$outh Street is the old name for the section of the Main Road between the 'Fox and Hounds' and Hawley Corner. The stretch shown in this picture is easily identified today, but the flint cottages to the left are no longer there, having been demolished after suffering severe bomb damage during the Second World War.

58. 'BUCKHURST LODGE', WESTERHAM HILL

*A*lthough the two wings are almost certainly mid-nineteenth century additions, the central part of 'Buckhurst Lodge' is a former building of some antiquity having been a hunting lodge associated with the Manor of Aperfield. The building still has much the same appearance now as it did when this picture was taken about 1910.

59. PROFESSOR AND MRS. CARLTON JOHN LAMBERT

*P*rofessor Lambert and his wife took up residence at 'Buckhurst Lodge' in 1909, after his retirement from the Royal Naval College at Greenwich where he had been Professor of Mathematics for thirty-six years. They took a keen interest in local organisations, like the Cudham Common Weal Society and were founders of the Cudham and District Nursing Association for which regular fund-raising events were held in the grounds of 'Buckhurst Lodge'. Professor and Mrs. Lambert are seen here by the 'Buckhurst Stall' on one such occasion. The lady on the right however has spoiled the picture by turning her head at the wrong moment.

60. GROUP IN THE GROUNDS OF 'BUCKHURST LODGE'

$\mathscr{A}$n elegant group of Edwardian ladies and gentlemen are joined by Professor Lambert (left) for a photograph during one of the events held at 'Buckhurst Lodge'. The rather incongruous piano, used to accompany a dancing display in which three young ladies in white had taken part, did not appear on the postcard which was published of the picture. Professor Lambert died on 6th November 1921, just one month before he and his wife would have celebrated their Golden Wedding, and was buried in the churchyard at Keston.

61. THE BAPTIST CHAPEL, SOUTH STREET

*T*he occasion pictured here is the opening of the rebuilt Chapel for public worship on 6th September 1911 by Mr. G. H. Dean, J.P., of Sittingbourne and Miss Dean, who have just performed the ceremony of unlocking the door. Road widening and the construction of a Hall and car park in recent years have combined to make considerable changes in the view as seen today.

62. ST. WINIFRED'S ROAD

$\mathcal{S}$omebody's spelling leaves much to be desired as did the surface of this road for many years. In 1923 a coal lorry, stuck in the mud and ruts, overheated and caught fire calling for the attendance of a fire appliance from the R.A.F. Station. The view here, looking towards the Main Road, can still be recognised quite easily.

63. 'THE WHITE HOUSE', ST. WINIFRED'S ROAD

$\mathcal{M}$rs. Carlton John Lambert, following the death of her husband, left 'Buckhurst Lodge' and moved into 'The White House', which formerly stood on the corner of St. Winifred's Road and Moselle Road. The illustration is a postcard used by Mrs. Lambert to send a New Year Greeting in 1922. She remained active in the village for some years and laid one of the foundation stones at the Aperfield Women's Institute Hall, Lebanon Gardens, in July 1932.

64. SHAKESPEARE AT 'TREDINNOCK'

𝒯he Aperfield Women's Institute was a flourishing organisation in the village long before their hall was built in Lebanon Gardens, meetings being held in the Beacon Hall or St. Mark's Church Hall. Here a group of players pause for a photograph during an open air performance of *The Merchant of Venice* in the grounds of 'Tredinnock', Sutherland Avenue, home of the local W.I. president, Mrs. Wheeler.

65. JUNCTION OF SUTHERLAND AVENUE AND EDWARD ROAD

In this picture we can see the early stages of road deterioration. Grass and weeds grow on the rolled chalk surface and ruts are being carved out by the wheels of heavy vehicles. Edward Road goes off to the right, the bungalow on the corner being 'The Summit' and, immediately to the left, is the start of the footpath known as 'Jacob's Ladder'.

66. 'SUNBURY', EDWARD ROAD

$\mathcal{T}$his was the home for many years of Miss I. K. Berridge, sometime president of the Aperfield Women's Institute, Governor of Biggin Hill Council School, devoted worker for St. Mark's Church and an enthusiastic beekeeper. The house which stood on the corner of Edward Road and Moselle Road, and which had a large and picturesque garden, was demolished around 1965 to make way for denser housing development.

SUTHERLAND AVENUE

67. SUTHERLAND AVENUE

This scene was located where the footpath, known as the 'Cinder Path' on one side and the 'Pinewoods' on the other, crosses Sutherland Avenue. Both the buildings in the photograph have been demolished. To the right is 'Heather Bank', later used during the Battle of Britain as a dormitory for R.A.F. pilots, and to the left the coach house and stable belonging to 'Highclere'.

68. VIEW FROM SUTHERLAND AVENUE TO ST. MARK'S CHURCH

$\mathcal{I}$t is very easy to see from this photograph, taken from the Polesteeple end of Sutherland Avenue, what a commanding position the first St. Mark's Church occupied over the valley and surrounding countryside. The two houses in the foreground, since demolished, were known as 1 and 2 Sutherland Avenue. In the one on the left lived Arthur Hankins, who, as a young man, maintained a smallholding on the adjoining land.

69. ARTHUR EDWARD HANKINS ('DUMMY')

One of a number of 'characters' frequently encountered in the Biggin Hill of bygone days was 'Dummy', a man of formidable appearance yet amiable disposition. Deaf and dumb, but always with something to 'say' he would first try sign language, accompanied by strange guttural sounds made through ill-fitting false teeth. Failure to comprehend meant waiting whist he traced out the letters of each word with a matchstick on a matchbox. He died on 2nd January 1962.

70. 'MAES-YR-HAF', MOUNT PLEASANT

This picture is typical of a great many taken by W. H. Nelson of subsequently demolished bungalows in Biggin Hill, with their owners proudly posed outside. House numbering did not come to Biggin Hill until the early 1950s, before which all properties were given names. This one, loosely translated from the Welsh, means 'Summer Field'.

71. 'THE HOLLIES', HILLCREST ROAD

*T*his bungalow, which had fine views over the valley, was the home of horse-bus driver Bill Salmon (seen in **26**) and his family and also of Mr. W. ('Uncle') Bellingham (seen in **145** and **147**). Outside the bungalow are Bill Salmon's parents and his son Jack.

THE VALLEY
CUDHAM

72. STOCK HILL AND ' IVY COTTAGE'

*T*he principal approach road to the valley has always been Stock Hill on which this photograph was taken about 1907 from a point near the end of what is now Merryhills Close. The three people at the foot of the hill are standing roughly in the middle of the present-day roundabout. Note the position of the former 'Ivy Cottage' on the flat bottom of the valley as a guide to the location of several of the pictures which follow.

73. STOCK HILL

*T*he picture here was probably taken at the same time and place as the previous one, but with the camera turned to face uphill instead of down. Apart from the installation of a few gas lamps and improvement to the road surface, Stock Hill changed very little until major works were commenced in 1970 to meet the needs of the growing population of the valley.

74. 'TROY', STOCK HILL AND MOUNT PLEASANT

Standing alone at the foot of Stock Hill, and having the appearance of a pioneer settlement stockaded against attack by the Apaches, is 'Troy' one of the earliest of Biggin Hill's buildings which still survives today. Behind it, a bleak Mount Pleasant rises up and, at the top, between the clumps of trees, is the Refreshment and Auction Room of the Aperfield Court Estate.

75. 'ANN'S COTTAGE' AND 'VALE COTTAGES'

*I*t would be hard to find a picture which conveys, better than this one, the still and lonely atmosphere of the valley on a cold winter's day in the very early years of the last century. 'Vale Cottages' are on the right and in the distance, just above 'Ann's Cottage', the home of Mr. A. F. Bushell, is Jugs Hill. As yet there are no buildings to be seen in Sunningvale Avenue or at the Jugs Hill end of Hillcrest Road.

76. LOOKING UP FROM THE VALLEY TO ST. MARK'S CHURCH (1)

Stock Hill winds its way up through the trees to the right of the picture with Hillcrest Road top left, and St. Marks in the centre. The dark hedge in the foreground is along Norheads Lane with 'Ivy Cottage' on the right. Painted on the roof of a bungalow in Hillcrest Road is a trade advertisement reading 'J. KENSIT & SONS. ESTIMATES GIVEN FOR ALL KINDS OF BUILDING & GLAZING'.

77. LOOKING UP FROM THE VALLEY TO ST. MARK'S CHURCH (2)

$\mathcal{A}$ later picture than the last one, but taken from a similar position with Stock Hill in the centre. A number of new buildings have appeared and note how quickly the growing trees and bushes are changing the landscape. To the left of 'Vale Cottages' a South Suburban Co-operative Society's delivery van is being driven carefully along Norheads Lane.

78. LOOKING UP FROM THE VALLEY TO ST. MARK'S CHURCH (3)

*A*nother photograph from a similar position to the last two, but taken in the early 1920s. Even more buildings can now be seen on the hillside. To the right, the fuselage of an R.A.F. aircraft suffers the final indignity of being placed on end in someone's garden and used to support a clothes line.

79. LOOKING UP MELROSE ROAD TO HILLCREST ROAD

*A*nother 1920s picture shows much of the hillside seen in **75** after the arrival of a considerable amount of random development. Melrose Road is the track to the left, terminating at the foot of Jugs Hill. The large bungalow built on the hillside immediately above was 'Normanhurst', for many years occupied by Mr. Braggar, a well-known local gardener and beekeeper.

80. CHALK PIT, SUNNINGVALE AVENUE

There is no evidence of it to be seen today, but over a century ago there was a chalk pit cut into the bank just to the Stock Hill side of Jugs Hill. This was later filled in and terraced as part of the garden of 'Normanhurst'.

81. JUGS HILL

'The Woods, Biggin Hill' may have been an appropriate title for a view of the lower section of Jugs Hill at that time, but not any longer. The path at this point in now flanked by railings and brick walls and overlooked by blocks of flats, in the building of which most of the trees seen in the picture were felled.

82. FIRST WORLD WAR ARMY LORRIES IN SUNNINGVALE AVENUE

One wonders who was foolhardy enough to order a convoy of First World War army vehicles to travel along the length of Sunningvale Avenue between Christy and Melrose Roads. This section became a regular venue for motor-cycle trials in the early 1930s, giving rise to violent scenes between the riders and local residents.

83. VIEW OVER ARTHUR ROAD AND SUNNINGVALE AVENUE UP TO HILL FIELD

$\mathcal{A}$ great many of the early Biggin Hill buildings have been demolished over the years to make way for new housing, but 'The Hermitage', 30 Arthur Road (bottom left) and semi-detached 'Rosalie' and 'Glenarden', 27 and 29 Sunningvale Avenue (top centre) are among those that have survived. 'Sunningvale Bungalow' (centre right) is now gone but some of the little conifers which can be seen here planted on its right hand boundary have now grown into very tall trees.

84. UPPER END OF SUNNINGVALE AVENUE (1)

$\mathcal{T}$his photograph of about 1908 shows the stretch of Sunningvale Avenue from Christy Road up to the Main Road. Intensive property development has taken place in this area, one of the older properties which was demolished being 'Hall's Canadian Poultry Farm' to the centre right of the picture.

85. HALL'S CANADIAN POULTRY FARM

𝒯he board to the left of the house reads 'C. HALL, CONTRACTOR, FENCIN DONE, OAK POSTS &WIRE, BIGGIN HILL, KENT. SAW SHARPENED'. Under the verandah peacocks are to be seen among the Hall family and their visitors as they pose for the photographer.

86. MR AND MRS. C. HALL

$\mathcal{S}$een here on a working day are Mr. and Mrs. Hall standing in the grounds of the 'Canadian Poultry Farm' with children posing on a haystack and with a notice between them reading 'Harvest Home 1910'. The girl in the centre rests her hand on a basket of eggs whilst Mrs. Hall holds a bin of corn to scatter among the chickens.

The Valley   Biggin Hill

87. UPPER END OF SUNNINGVALE AVENUE (2)

*T*his is a similar view to **84**, but the date is about ten years later, after the erection of several new bungalows above and below Sunningvale Avenue. The large white bungalow left of centre called 'The Turret' was built after the First World War by a local ex-servicemen's building co-operative called *The Ferrate*. The enterprise soon ran into financial difficulties and went out of business.

88. CAPTAIN URIAH COOKE AT 'TREVOSE'

'Trevose', seen in the top right hand corner of the last picture, was the home of Captain Uriah Cooke, and was at one time in the occasional occupation of the eminent politician and Prime Minister, David Lloyd-George. Captain Cooke, photographed here at 'Trevose', was one of the locals sworn in as a Special Constable in 1914 and was probably 'Barnacle Bill', who, as is mentioned in *R.A.F. Biggin Hill* by Graham Wallace, had by 1918 attached himself to the Officers Mess on the Station.

89. WRAFS OF WORLD WAR I

$\mathcal{B}$y 1918, the strength at R.A.F. Biggin Hill was 593, including 228 WRAFS. Among those recruited locally were Blanche Castle of Mount Pleasant (left) and Christine Nelson, daughter of the photographer, seen here 'taking afternoon tea'. They were volunteers for clerical duties and worked as typists in the Station Office.

90. VIEW ALONG SUNNINGVALE AVENUE TO MOUNT PLEASANT

𝒯he small trees in the foreground of this photograph have now grown to such an extent as to block out this tranquil view along Sunningvale Avenue, over Christy Road, Melrose Road, Stock Hill and up to Mount Pleasant in the far distance. This was one of the best-selling of the Biggin Hill view postcards produced by W. H. Nelson.

91. VIEW OVER MELROSE AND ARTHUR ROADS TO OAKLANDS LANE

*I*n the foreground is 'Trafalgar Bungalow' built by W. H. Nelson in 1903. Note the flag pole at the rear and the bell tent in the field at a spot now lost among homes and gardens. The part of the field known as Little Stock in the foreground is now the site of Keymer Close. Great Stock began on the far side of Melrose Road.

92. EARLY MORNING IN CAMP

*T*aken from among the trees on the bank near Jugs Hill before the clearance of
the early morning mist, this photograph of about 1906 shows a Church Lads' Brigade
Camp on the land between Arthur Road and Oaklands Lane. The bungalow to the
right is 'Three Gables', later the country home of Sir Arthur Newsholme, K.C.B., who
until 1919 was Principal Medical Officer to the Local Government Board.

93. MR. ROLLA RICHARDS

*M*r, Richards, one of Biggin Hill's early eccentrics, was often seen, as in this photograph, riding his tricycle with a black cat perched on his shoulder. He lived at 'Woodville', Melrose Road, the white bungalow on the right of picture **91**. He died in 1931 and by his Will left £500 to Cudham Church. The bequest was used to purchase three additional bells and to install the striking clock in the church tower.

94. VALE COTTAGES AND LOWER TEMPLE'S

$\mathcal{F}$rom low on the bank sloping up to Mount Pleasant we look over Vale Cottages to Arthur Road and to Victoria Gardens beyond. The square wooden building on the right is Temple's 'bottom shop'. The little white bungalow in the centre of the photograph was built by Harry Nelson in 1921 and it was in the garden shed here that the negatives from which most of the photographs in this book were made were stored from 1945 to 1975.

95. 'THE RAMBLERS', MELROSE ROAD

𝒥ust to the left of Harry Nelson's bungalow in the last photograph is this one built by a Mr. Cole, By the time the picture was taken a glass verandah had been added at the front. The distinctive Biggin Hill character on the right of the group is 'Champagne Charlie' Elbourne, whose home was a short way down Arthur Road.

96. *VIEW FROM STOCK HILL TO THE UPPER END OF SUNNINGVALE AVENUE*

*T*here could be no better caption than the one below written by 'Fred' in 1917 on the back of a postcard bearing this picture.

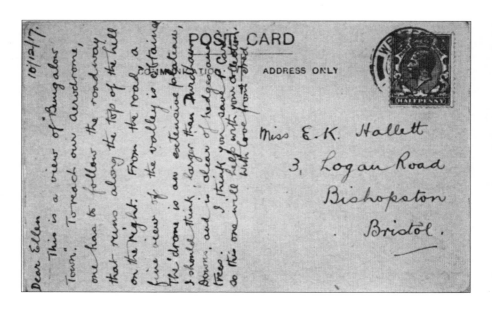

97. 'RYDAL', CHRISTY ROAD

ere we see a wooden bungalow built in the very best traditions of early Biggin Hill. Note the elegantly carved fascia board and the fine workmanship which has gone into the construction of the porch. Decorative fences like this, with a gate to match, are now entirely out of fashion. Just to the right of where the bungalow stood, there is now a modern house which has retained the name 'Rydal'.

98. VICTORIA GARDENS

*F*rom a position high up on Sunningvale Avenue, in about 1906, we look down over Victoria Gardens and Oaklands Lane to the Norheads Farm field known as West Hill Bottom. The house at the corner of the Lane is 'The Glen' with its stable at the rear, and the existence of scaffolding and materials indicates that the building has only just been completed. There are some colourful local stories about royal associations with 'The Glen', which it would be ungracious to controvert.

99. VIEW OVER VICTORIA GARDENS TO OAKLANDS LANE

Old Biggin Hill residents love to relate their experiences during horrendous snowstorms in the past. Judging by the number of photographs taken in snow by W.H. Nelson it does seem that Biggin Hill suffers more from heavy snowfalls than many other places. Here the view is over the area from Victoria Gardens to Oaklands Lane with the end of Christy Road top left. Sheep, with their lambs are to be seen in the field called Great Hook.

100. 'THE CRIB', CHRISTY ROAD

𝒯his is a close-up of the bungalow seen in the last picture at the corner of Christy Road and Oaklands Lane, sometimes known as 'Cooper's Bungalow'. The typical summer house has been extended by means of flat roofed auditions at the sides and climbing roses are trained up trellis work to create a country cottage effect.

101. FAMILY GATHERING, VICTORIA GARDENS

$\mathcal{I}$t has been established, during the years since *Grandfather's Biggin Hill* was first published, that this fashionably dressed Edwardian group were brought together from as far away as Canada to celebrate the Golden Wedding Anniversary of Mr and Mrs Bath who are seated in the centre dressed in dark colours.

102. THE VALLEY FROM THE UPPER END OF SUNNINGVALE AVENUE

*A*nother W. H. Nelson snowscape, in which Oaklands Lane, with oak trees spaced out along it, cuts diagonally across the centre of the picture. Top right is Norheads Farm and top left, Swievelands. In the left foreground several rows of beehives stand in one of the gardens sloping down from Sunningvale Avenue.

103. NORHEADS FARMYARD

*N*orheads, known in much earlier times as Norwoods, Norrods or Norrads, is a farm with many historic connections standing at the top of the hill on the far side of Biggin Hill valley. The splendid Georgian farmhouse (just appearing to the right of the picture) was built in 1715 by John Glover.

104. THE MILK CART

$\mathcal{I}$n 1896, William Stone established, at Norheads Farm, the dairy which was to be the main supplier of milk and other dairy produce to the people of Biggin Hill for the next seventy years. After his death, around 1923, the business was continued by his son Albert. Before the days of milk bottles, the milk was ladled out by the milkman from a large churn carried round on a cart. Here, the milkman standing by the cart in Arthur Road, is Frank Watts.

105. CHURCH LADS' BRIGADE IN CAMP

The field now occupied by the Oaklands Schools was, in the early part of the last century, a popular site for the annual camps of units of the Church Lads' Brigade. They came mostly from the Croydon area and marched in both directions led by their drum and fife band. This view is from opposite the 'Black Horse' with Norheads Farm buildings top left.

106. THE CAMP HEADQUARTERS

*O*fficers and men form up for an official photograph outside the headquarters marquee, with drums, cymbals and rifles carefully arranged. The Church Lads' Brigade was conducted on strict military lines and in 1911 became officially recognised as an army cadet organisation. Many of the young men in this and the next picture would have joined an army unit, probably the King's Royal Rifle Corps, and been among the first to go to the front in the 1914-18 War, suffering heavy casualties.

107. A HOT DAY IN CAMP

$\mathcal{H}$ere we see a smaller group of members of the Church Lads' Brigade, photographed in the next field in 1909, wearing French Foreign Legion style headgear against the heat of the sun. The view to the rear of the group emphasises the open aspect of the Biggin Hill countryside at that time, without a building to be seen in Sunningvale Avenue, which crosses the picture horizontally below the line of trees. Jugs Hill is the straight path between the two open fields at the top centre.

108. VIEW OVER 'IVY COTTAGE' UP TO NORHEADS FARM

$\mathcal{I}$n this remarkable early picture, the thin chalk line is Kings Road, just planted with the poplar trees which, for many years afterwards, grew along much of its length. The dark line of bushes above is Highfield Road with 'Chelsea Villa' the house standing on the corner of Norheads Lane. In the foreground, opposite 'Ivy Cottage', workmen are loading hay on to a cart, but the days when farming was carried on in the valley were rapidly coming to an end.

109. VIEW OVER VALE COTTAGES TO KINGS ROAD

This photograph was taken at the same time as **108**, with the camera moved round slightly to the left. Between 'Vale Cottages' and 'Ivy Cottage' the old sheep sheds, formerly part of Bottom Barn Farm, can clearly be seen. Behind 'Ann's Cottage' on the opposite side of Norheads Lane an old railway wagon has been brought into use as an outbuilding.

110. VIEW OVER NORHEADS LANE TO KINGS ROAD AND HIGHFIELD ROAD

*I*n this later picture we see the left hand section of **108** from a slightly different angle, with Norheads Lane in the foreground. Kings Road is still the horizontal white line, but note how the poplar trees have matured and the way in which sporadic building has cluttered up the view. None of this is recognisable now, but the large house to the left in Kings Road, formerly known as 'Dunoon', was one of the longest to survive.

111. 'EASTERN VIEW', GRAND VIEW AVENUE

$\mathcal{B}$uilding this bungalow, seen in the top left hand corner of **110** and here in close-up, called for no more than a little ingenuity and two huts surplus to Army requirements after the First World War. On sloping ground, the use of detached piers like this, instead of excavating a flat surface, reduced dampness as well as providing some extra storage space underneath the building.

112. KINGS ROAD AND HIGHFIELD ROAD

*N*ot an easy section of Kings Road to identify nowadays, but the little white painted bungalow with the verandah on the left of the picture was, before its demolition, known as 52 Kings Road. The field in the centre, formerly known as Sheat Bank, is seen at an earlier time to the left hand side of **109**.

113. BOTTOM OF THE VALLEY

We are looking now from somewhere near the present site of The Roundways right along the bottom of the valley, with 'Vale Cottages ' to our left and 'Ivy Cottage' to our right. In the far distance we can see to Melody Road and beyond. The large ash tree on the left, known locally as 'Old Riley', stood at the side of Rosehill Road. When it was cut down, many years ago, the sound of it falling was heard at the 'Black Horse', half a mile away.

114. VIEW OF KINGS ROAD UP TO LONG COPPICE

$\mathcal{T}$his very popular W. H. Nelson postcard is one which, before the days of colour photography, was often sold hand-tinted in green, blue and red. Kings Road once again crosses the picture horizontally, with the site on which 'The Flying Machine' now stands over to the left. The dark line of trees crossing the centre of the picture diagonally marks the course of the bridle path from Rosehill Road up to Highfield Road.

115. MELODY ROAD

*A*nother view, like the last one, taken from Mount Pleasant looking down over Sunningvale Avenue, which can just be seen at the bottom of the picture after having turned the sharp left-hand bend near Rosehill Road. Melody Road cuts along the valley ahead of us and Kings Road with its tall poplar trees is on the right.

116. KINGS ROAD (1)

Without the benefit of the memories of old residents, it would be impossible to locate this spot now that the view is obscured by housing development. Just behind the trees on the right, the road bends at the junction with Spring Gardens and at the top of the bank is Beech Road, running along the edge of Long Coppice.

117. KINGS ROAD (2)

A stretch of the road quite close to the last one and again barely recognisable today among the tiers of town houses. The old lorry, XA 9667, with its engine removed, appears to have arrived at its final resting place.

118. VIEW OVER MELODY ROAD TO SWIEVELANDS

Swievelands Road skirts the wood at the top of the hill and Melody Road crosses the centre. Spring Gardens is just off the picture to the left. At £10 for a plot with a twenty foot frontage on to any road, the land seen in this photograph was among the cheapest to be found on the Aperfield Court Estate.

119. VIEW FROM SUNNINGVALE AVENUE UP TO ST. MARY'S GROVE

This section of Sunningvale Avenue between Melody and Swievelands Roads, was one of Mr. F. H. Dougal's new roads which did not follow an old field boundary. It cut through Glazing Bottom, the line of bushes across the centre being the boundary between that field and Round Grove Hill. The land in the centre of the picture is now the site of Churchside Close.

120. SWIEVELANDS

*H*ere we see the view looking from Mount Pleasant across the Valley to the area known as Swievelands. An earlier spelling of the name is used on the postcard. Previously it appeared on maps as Swiftlands or Swiflins. St. Mary's Grove runs along the edge of the wood at the top and the large bungalow over to the left is 'Gowan Brae' on the uphill side of Lillie Road.

121. PRIVATE TRANSPORT

*T*his smart little pony and trap provided a very suitable means of getting about Biggin Hill in the days when only a small minority were privileged to own a motor-car. The occupants from left to right are Lawson Ross, Margaret Ross, Mrs. Ross, Miss Anderson and Miss Goult, all of whom lived in Lillie Road.

122. THE 'SINGING COLONY'

$\mathcal{E}$arly in 1914 a bungalow in St. Mary's Grove was rented by Madame Clara Novello Davies, founder and conductor of the Royal Welsh Ladies' Choir and a singing teacher of considerable repute. Her idea was to bring her pupils to join her 'Singing Colony' in Biggin Hill where clean air, fresh natural foods and the wide open spaces would be beneficial to their artistic training and voice production. Local people looked on them with some curiosity and amusement, but they did not stay for long. At the first sound of the enemy overhead in the First World War they were gone. In this original W. H. Nelson postcard we see a group leaning over the fence of the bungalow, with Madame Clara third from the right. Next to her is her son, who was to become the famous Ivor Novello.

123. THE YOUNG IVOR NOVELLO WITH HIS 'MAM'

$\mathcal{B}$orn David Ivor Davies at Cardiff in 1893, Ivor Novello learned to play the piano well as a child and when a teenager he accompanied his mother's choir as well as playing for the lessons at her London studio. He came to Biggin Hill in 1914 with the 'Singing Colony' and lived in his own Romany caravan in the grounds of the bungalow in St. Mary's Grove. It was at this time that he composed *Keep the Home Fires Burning* which was published late in 1914 and became the most popular song of the First World War. In this previously unpublished photograph, Ivor Novello is seen at St. Mary's Grove with his 'Mam' who was a major influence on his later career in the theatre.

124. *THE GROVE AND 'DEADMAN'S BANK' FROM LILLIE ROAD*

*T*here are several stories of murder and tragic death associated with Biggin Hill, few being founded on reliable fact. One concerns a man found hanged on the wooded slope between Sutherland Avenue, at the top of the picture, and The Grove below. The name 'Deadman's Bank' is however derived from Denman's Bottom the old name for the field through which The Grove was constructed.

125. BUNGALOW IN SUNNINGVALE AVENUE

*T*his was originally thought to be 'Surrey View' The Grove, to which it bore a remarkable resemblance and probably shared the same builder, but has now been identified as the bungalow in Sunningvale Avenue seen on the left of **82**. Complete wooden buildings of this kind could be purchased in prefabricated sections and delivered to the site for assembly.

126. POLESTEEPLE HILL

𝒯he scene here, looking up Polesteeple Hill from a point just above the junction with The Grove has changed dramatically in recent years with the bank on the right being removed to create land suitable for housing development. The hill is still as steep as ever and many an ageing car will be grateful that only one-way traffic in a downward direction is now permitted. The origin of the name is not known, but any research would need to begin at least three hundred years ago.

127. MOUNT PLEASANT FROM SWIEVELANDS

We are actually looking in the opposite direction across the valley from a point somewhere in the middle of **120**. The gardens of the bungalows on the right slope down from Polesteeple Hill and the buildings at the top of the hill, towards the centre, are in Mount Pleasant. Around 1979 work began on the demolition of most of the bungalows seen here and the clearance of the land in preparation for extensive property development.

128. AN AFTERNOON OUT AT BIGGIN HILL

$\mathcal{H}$ere we find a group, rather formally dressed by present day standards, enjoying a peaceful afternoon at their bungalow on the bank above Sunningvale Avenue, opposite the junction with Melody Road. The building would have started with just a bare rectangular wooden shed with a corrugated iron roof to which the verandah at the front and the side extension were added later.

129. VIEW FROM SUNNINGVALE AVENUE UP TO MOUNT PLEASANT

$\mathcal{I}$n our final photograph of Biggin Hill valley, we see in the lower right hand corner a later view of the bungalow in the previous picture. The gates on the left open out on to Yew Tree Path, running from the foot of Polesteeple Hill to Rosehill Road, which formed part of the ancient bridle path between Aperfield and Norheads.

130. 'OLD LIZZIE' (MRS ELIZABETH LENNINGTON)

𝒯his elderly lady, who originally came from South Shields with her husband, worked for many years at Costains Farm in Jail Lane and when the farm was taken over by Mr. A. B. Gee, he allowed her to continue to live on the farm, rent free. When she died in the1930s, the expenses of her funeral were subscribed by local people and the coffin bearers were four airmen from the R.A.F. Station.

131. MR. ARTHUR MARKHAM, HIS CHILDREN AND HORSE

On the right stands farmer, Arthur Markham, with his daughter Edith and son Ernest, proudly displaying his horse *Darkie* which he purchased in 1908 for £100, a very considerable sum at that time. Mr Markham farmed at Hosletts, Jail Lane, on land which is now occupied by the Charles Darwin School.

132. 'THE OLD JAIL'

' $\mathcal{F}$ ox & Sons' Oak Brewery at Green Street Green closed down in 1908 and 'The Old Jail' was one of their properties sold by auction on 15th June 1909. This picture, taken around that time, shows that the inn was formerly a pair of cottages and still had their two front doors. The origin of the name is uncertain, but probably refers back to a time, long ago, when prisoners being taken from London to Maidstone Jail were accommodated there overnight. It became a beer shop in 1869 and a public-house four years later. In 1895, the Landlord, Richard Cowlard, was also the proprietor of a bakery on the premises.

133. PARADE TO CUDHAM CHURCH

$\mathcal{L}$ined up along the roadside from 'The Old Jail' back towards Cudham School, is a parade of mostly younger members of St. Mark's Church as they process towards Cudham Church. The year is about 1909, and leading the parade bearing the Union Jack is Mr. Burton Aves, a well known figure in Biggin Hill for many years. Immediately behind him is the then Curate-in-Charge of St. Mark's, the Rev. W. F. Hamilton. They are followed by the four sidesmen, from left to right Messrs. Cornell, Hallam, Stone and Bushell.

134. THE VICAR OF CUDHAM AND HIS CURATE, 1906

The Vicar of Cudham from 1898 to 1915 was the Rev. Harold Augustus Curtis, the son of an Orpington doctor. He is seen standing on the left of this picture, taken at the door of Cudham Church. Seated is the Rev. Alfred Ashton, Curate-in-Charge of St. Mark's Aperfield, who was accommodated at 'Whitecliff', Sutherland Avenue. The house, later occupied by the schoolmaster, Mr. Walter Crooks, still survives.

135. EMPIRE DAY 1905, CUDHAM SCHOOL, JAIL LANE

*T*he only school in the Parish of Cudham during the early years of the twentieth century, apart from a small one at Fairchildes, was the Church of England School in Jail Lane which opened in 1873. For many children, especially those living in the valley at Biggin Hill, it was a long and rough walk to school and home again each day. For even the smallest child a pair of strong hobnail boots, such as those seen along the front row in the picture, was an absolute necessity.

136. EMPIRE DAY 1908, CUDHAM SCHOOL, JAIL LANE

*A*t school, Empire Day used to be the most popular day of the year. Celebrated on 24th May (Queen Victoria's birthday) everyone arrived in their best clothes, sang hymns, 'Rule Britannia' and the National Anthem, joined in a pageant or flag waving parade and then had the rest of the day off. What better occasion could there be to invite the school photographer to come in and take the annual photographs? In the previous picture it will be seen that the children are wearing hats and the teacher, Miss Blundell, is not. Here the children are hatless, giving the mistress a chance to show off her fashionable creation.

137. EMPIRE DAY 1913, CUDHAM SCHOOL, JAIL LANE

The garden of the School House is the setting for this Empire Day photograph, the last in which several of the more senior children were to appear before being transferred to the new Council School at Biggin Hill. The names of most of the children are known, and on the right is Mr. Walter Crooks, who had been headmaster of the school since 1886. On the far left, the mistress is Edith Cornell, who was to be married four months later. For more details of the children's names see the Appendix on page 179.

138. *THE WEDDING OF BURTON AVES AND EDITH CORNELL*

On 18th September 1913, Burton Aves (seen in **133**) and Edith Cornell (seen in **137**) were married at Cudham Parish Church by the Rev. H. A. Curtis and the reception was held at 'Charnwood', Main Road, Biggin Hill, the Cornell family home. In this wedding group the bridesmaids on the left are sisters of the bridegroom and on the right those of the bride. The bride's parents stand behind her and the bridegroom's mother is the lady dressed all in black. The guests on the left are Mrs. Carlton Lambert, Mrs. Crooks and Mr. Crooks. Mrs. Arthur Tremain of 'Mead House' is on the far right. The well-built lady in the white hat looking away into the distance is Mrs. Milbank of 'The Mill House'.

139. HAROLD AVES

$\mathcal{T}$he best man at the wedding of his brother Burton (seen back right in the last photograph) was a first class athlete, as evidenced by the fine collection of prizes he proudly displays here. As a middle distance runner Harold Aves particularly excelled, but he competed in other events as well. On August Bank Holiday, 1909, he was first in the one mile 'Round the Village' race at Downe and won a similar race at Knockholt sports two weeks later. On that day however, he was beaten into second place in the High Jump by his brother Burton.

140. MR. WALTER CROOKS

From 1886 to 1914, Walter Crooks was headmaster of Cudham School in Jail Lane. He also served the community as the first Clerk to the Parish Council from 1895, and as church organist and Choir Master. He is seen here with teachers Miss Simpson and Mrs. Dover, shortly after taking up the post of headmaster at the new Biggin Hill Council School in 1914. Mr. Crooks died in 1926 aged 62.

141. BIGGIN HILL COUNCIL SCHOOL, 1914

$\mathcal{T}$he many local people who as children attended Biggin Hill School will recognise that this photograph was taken underneath the verandah of the building seen in the preceding picture **140**. When the school opened on 20th May 1914 it had a total of one hundred and nineteen pupils including forty-four infants. Here we see the senior class most of whom had previously attended Cudham School, Jail Lane. For more information on the children's names see the Appendix on page 179.

142. BEST ATTENDANCE CLASS, BIGGIN HILL SCHOOL

 *N*ot a truant among them last week, so this Class was awarded the banner held by Ray Wallis on the right. But what made it an occasion for a photograph? Perhaps it was a distinction they did not often achieve! It is odd, too, that at a co-educational school there was not a girl to be seen on this cold, wet day around 1915.

143. THE ALLOTMENTS, BIGGIN HILL SCHOOL, ABOUT 1920

*T*he strip of land between 'The Haven' and 'Highclere' on which the school canteen was later built, was for many years the boys' allotments. There were about eight plots and throughout each growing season practical instruction in vegetable cultivation was given. Percy Bayes is on the far left, Harold Blake to the right of centre and next to him, shouldering his fork, is Frank Tremain.

144. PUBLIC MEETING AT BIGGIN HILL COUNCIL SCHOOL

We have seen in **140** the outside of Biggin Hill School. Here we catch a glimpse of the inside when it is being used as a public meeting hall. It may possibly have been the occasion on 16th September 1922 when the 'deeds' of Biggin Hill Green were handed over at a specially convened meeting of the Cudham Parish Council (see **18**). Those attending sit, in some apparent discomfort, at desks designed for much smaller beings. The school at this time seems to have been one large room, but folding partitions were installed later allowing it to be divided into three classrooms.

145. *BIGGIN HILL FOOTBALL TEAM, ABOUT 1919.*

*T*his is a good example of a photograph where the old residents approached failed to agree on the names to go with each of the faces. The best consensus however is *(Back row)* Fred Tremain, Mr. W. ('Uncle') Bellingham, the Rev. H. M. Woodward (Curate of St. Mark's), Jimmy Emptage, Jack Dewberry, Alf Hunt and Mr. Jim Blake. *(Front row)* Bill Blake, Frank Gee, Bill Whitehead, Stan Friend, Bill Ingleton, Ray Forbes and Ernie Blake. The ground on which the team played was at Costains Meadow, Jail Lane.

146. THE CHILDREN'S GYM CLASS, 1922

$\mathcal{P}$hotographed on the grassy slope behind the old St. Mark's Church, the Gym Class conducted by Miss Gwen Smith *(Back right)* was held in the Church Hall on the left, the pianist being Miss Horlock *(Back centre)*. The members of the class are *(Third row)* Binda Goldsborough, Dorothy Pyne, Ivy Abbott, Kathleen Bayes, Phyllis Crooks, May Hill, Gladys Tremain, Evelyn Hart and Ruth Terry. *(Second row)* Margaret Ross, Ivy Armstead, Nancy Hill, Herbert Gammon, James Crooks, Ken Smith, Derek Waters and Guy Goldsburgh. *(Front row)* Dorothy Pankhurst, Joyce Drew and Lawson Ross.

147. 1ST BIGGIN HILL SCOUTS AND ROVERS

Who would believe that this photograph of around 1916 was taken in the middle of what today is the car park behind Barclays Bank? Previously the grounds of Mr. Francis Vant's refreshment rooms, it was from 1912 the garden of The Beacon Stores, owned by Mr. Allchin. In the centre is the Scoutmaster, Mr. Wellings who was confined to a wheelchair and lived at 'Ashbourne' in Lebanon Gardens and behind him is his assistant, Mr. W. ('Uncle') Bellingham.

148. 1ST BIGGIN HILL SCOUT GROUP ON THE MAIN ROAD

$\mathcal{T}$he scoutmaster on the far right, in this picture taken about five years after the preceding one, is Mr. Gee outside whose garage the group is lined up. Now the site of a terrace of modern houses, it was then the Cudham & District Motor Transport and Power Co. where Biggin Hill's first fire engine was built and was garaged from 1931. The house seen through the trees is the old Post Office which stood opposite the Church Road junction with the Main Road.

149. THE FIRST HORTICULTURAL SHOW, 1923

𝒯he Cudham, Biggin Hill and District Horticultural and Fanciers Association was founded in 1922, and their first show was held on 6th August 1923, in the grounds of the new Central Hall Baptist Chapel, Main Road. The girl in white, standing next to Mrs. Carlton Lambert, is the photographer's youngest daughter, Vera Nelson, whose brother Harry won first prize in the Show for sweet peas and third prize for marrows. Jack Tessier, the boy in the cap, won prizes in the junior section and was closely connected with the Society until his death in 1971. Awards bearing his name are now competed for at the Society's Spring Show.

150. GREETINGS FROM BIGGIN HILL

$\mathcal{F}$inally, a rare example of the only 'multi-view' greetings postcard ever published by W. H. Nelson. Having commissioned the artwork, which measured about 18"x12", he mounted five of his own views on it and photographed it to make a 6½" x 4¾" negative from which he could print the postcards. This type of card has always been popular at seaside resorts and other holiday centres, but did not have a great appeal in Biggin Hill during the early 1920s.

APPENDIX

The following are lists are the best consensus of the names taken from information supplied by old Biggin Hill residents.

Picture **137**. EMPIRE DAY 1913, CUDHAM SCHOOL, JAIL LANE - see page 163

(Back row) Miss E. Cornell, Dulcie Crooks, not known, Evelyn Bayes, Nellie Batchelor, Bob Jackson and Mr. W. Crooks. *(Middle row)* Dorothy Drew, Alice Beagley, Ivy Cope and Millie Palethorpe *(Front row)* Fred Skinner, Stanley Nelson, not known, not known, Wally Watts and Harold Drew.

Picture **141**. BIGGIN HILL COUNCIL SCHOOL 1914 - see page 167

(Back row) May Temple, Hilda Gee, Dorothy Bayes, Hilda Abraham, Dulcie Crooks, Edith Hallam, Christine Nelson and Fred Skinner. *(Third row)* Len Allchin, George Lettington, Jack Salmon, Ted Hope, not known, and Alf Chilman. *(Second row)* Albert Shrubb, Norman Gee, Bill Sturrock, Henry Tobias, Wally Watts, Jim Beagley and Leslie Chilman. *(Front row)* Jack Tremain, Winnie Wicking, Millie Palethorpe and Dorothy Budgen.

INDEX

All numbers are pages not pictures.
References to illustrations are in bold.

H

O

P

R